It's Your Fucking Turn To Cook

IT'S YOUR FUCKING TURN TO COOK

A compendium of gentle tips and straightforward recipes for those who never seem to help out in the kitchen

MRS DEIDRE GAY-ABEL, DFG.

Buon-Cattivi Press
Adelaide, Australia

Published by the Buon-Cattivi Press, 2018
Adelaide, Australia

Copyright © Deidre Gay-Abel, 2018
All rights reserved.

ISBN 978-0-9953661-6-9

Printed by IngramSpark

Welcome to the *It's Your Fucking Turn To Cook* cookbook from Mrs Deidre Gay-Abel, DFG.

This cookbook, all its delicious recipes and additional instructions are dedicated to my husband Mr Theodore Abel, without whom I would never have reached the point of having to fucking write all this shit down. Here's to me having a night off from the kitchen. My hope is that it will serve my sister and brother DFGs as well.

CONTENTS

The contents of this cookbook are separated into a few simple sections to help guide even the most kitchen-illiterate of you through the Mrs Deidre Gay-Abel's *It's Your Fucking Turn To Cook* cookbook.

Navigating the cookbook: *INTRODUCTIONS*	1
General safety: *OFFERINGS & QUESTIONS*	7
How to make sure the food goes down well: *THE DRINKS*	13
All we have is ingredients, where's the food? *BASIC COOKING STUFF*	21
Freshly laid: *EGGS*	31
How long has that been there? *TINNED & DRY FOOD*	37
Does this smell right? *USING FRESHISH STUFF*	45
Where to finish: *SWEET THINGS*	57
Fuck! They're here. Now what? *DEALING WITH GUESTS*	65
Where was that fucking recipe again? *INDEX/LIST OF RECIPES*	71

Navigating the cookbook:

INTRODUCTIONS

INTRODUCING *IT'S YOUR F*CKING TURN TO COOK*

If you've received this book, perhaps as a gift from your more significant other, then there are a number of kitchen experiences that I imagine you're familiar with. Struggling to work out what ingredients to throw together for a meal, or being told off when you ask what to cook, are common experiences for at least fifty percent of people in a domestic relationship, so please don't feel utterly ashamed at your predicament. Luckily for you, help is at hand.

The *It's Your Fucking Turn To Cook* cookbook conveniently collates my forty-odd years of experience as a Domestic Fucking Goddess (DFG) to provide all the information you need to perform like a functioning adult in the kitchen, rather than acting like an intolerable twat. Each recipe is a complete set of instructions to prepare a straightforward meal, as I would usually respond to the phrase 'I don't know what to cook'.

Predictably, some readers will still have some reservations and apprehensions about the prospect of making their own way in the kitchen, and I've found the best advice for you is to fucking suck it up. You've had years of experience eating food lovingly prepared for you, so you should already know how it should look and how it should taste. Now you have this cookbook and the opportunity to get as much experience as you want. You are set to fucking cook. So tell the DFG who usually cooks your meals to rest easy as you'll do dinner tonight, and get your arse into the kitchen.

General safety:

OFFERINGS & QUESTIONS

We all need a little help here and there. There's no shame in that, unless you're asking the exact same goddamn question for years and refused to remember the answer. Don't fret, there is a way to get around these questions in this neat section on *Offerings & Questions.*

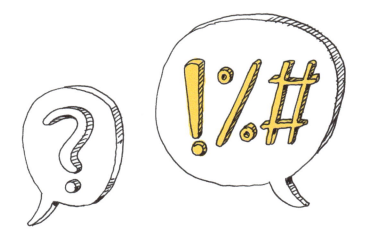

THE OFFERING

The offering is an essential component in the process of seeking assistance. Whenever asking an exhausted DFG any questions about cooking (or how to perform any domestic art, for that matter) an offering must be made.

I recommend that you make your offering generous to ensure satisfaction even if your cooking should prove inedible. I'm partial to wine or savoury foods, but apply your own personal knowledge of the DFG in question for best results.

When making an offering, or attempting the incredibly risky *Frequently Asked Question*, you must never turn your back on your DFG, especially if they hold the title of spouse, and so have had to put up with your bullshit for a long time. Always present the offering accompanied by a compliment before doing anything else, and you may then ask one concise question. Usually one to two offerings per night is acceptable. Once the offering is completed remember not to turn your back as you slowly step out of the room, your continued deference is necessary to ensure ongoing assistance to complete what should be a basic task.

Double Offerings

If you are unsure whether your standard offering will be sufficient it can be doubled. For example, if you need to ask where to find something in the kitchen the offering will need to be doubled. The double offering will go some way to make up for the fact that you were too lazy or frazzled to look for it properly yourself. For fuck's sake, it's in the fucking kitchen along with all the other kitchen things.

Frequently Asked Questions

For the kitchen-illiterate, the endless parade of wonderful meals that appear on the dinner table may create the appearance that your DFG is a fountain of cooking knowledge. While it is true that your DFG is an astonishing creature, it is simply not worth the risk to pester them with questions on the one night you step into the kitchen. Some useful advice I can offer here is to just google it. It is vastly more valuable to you to not piss off your DFG, and has the added bonus of making you look competent enough to do something for yourself, like a grown-up. Seriously, fucking google it.

Finishing Yourself Off

A common mistake among the kitchen-illiterate is to think that all the work is done once the meal is on the plate. Until you develop your skills in the kitchen, your cooking efforts will create an unholy amount of mess. It is essential for the harmony of the household that you always remember to clean up the mess you have caused. Until you spend as much time in the kitchen as your DFG, you are an intruder here, and the harsh punishment for any breaches will be greatly deserved. Some useful advice is to frequently clean up while you are cooking, or if it's easier for you to remember, don't be an inconsiderate cunt.

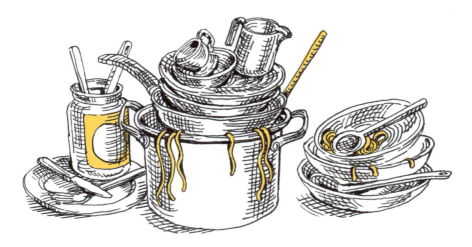

*How to make sure
the food goes down well:*

THE DRINKS

Every meal needs to be filling, delicious, and satisfying overall. A badly kept cook's secret in the presentation of a meal is the role played by drinks, especially the wonderfully versatile alcoholic beverage, which Mr Abel says 'sometimes also goes in the food'. He's not far off. Any meal can be made great by the drink it is consumed with. The more drinks applied, the less detail diners will notice about the food. Plan ahead and respond as required. If something's a little burned, pour an extra glass per person.

ALCOHOLIC DRINKS

Alcoholic beverages are the sort that can make any meal taste great. Applying the right amount to your DFG or guests will create a positive disposition and disguise any of your missteps in cooking. However, beware not to apply too much or your food will be tasted once again on the way back up. Trust me, it will be your food, not the alcohol blamed.

Wines

White wines allegedly pair well with lighter meats like chicken and fish, but really there are no fucking rules here. You're better off pairing your wines to the taste of your DFG and your guests rather than the food you serve. Serve chilled, if you haven't worked that out already. White wine is also a useful way for your DFG to relax after a day of managing household stressors, and a spontaneous offering of wine or a similar gesture will win you points. Rosé and moscato are good options if you're not good at wine.

Red wines are usually reserved for red meat, but again whatever floats your boat. Reds are also a better option in the chillier months, as it's served at room temperature. If you're keen to appear fancy in front of your friends, one option is to use a device to aerate the wine and serve it in a fancy wine decanter. Hopefully your DFG will let you know if you start to look too much like a wanker.

Ports are most appropriately served after all the food has been eaten, and are a useful way to let guests know it will soon be time to fuck off home. However, if the quality of port is too high, guests may not receive this message. Results may vary.

Beers & Ciders

Beer and cider are another beverage option, and should be included if that better suits the tastes of your guests or DFG. I'd like to assume that I don't need to provide instructions here, but I probably can't, so make sure that you keep some chilled in the fridge, or immerse them in ice if you need to chill them quickly. To really impress people with your thoughtfulness and preparation, have a bottle opener handy.

Pirlo

Making cocktails is a valuable skill that deserves a book of its own (hint hint, Mr Publisher), but here's one to get you started. Pirlo is an easy cocktail for a workday afternoon. It's supposed to be cheap and refreshing, so if you're using fancy wine you're doing it wrong. Mix as follows:

 One shot (use a shot glass or espresso cup) of Aperol.

 Three shots of shitty white wine (the less flavour the better).

 Heaps of ice and soda water to fill the glass up.

If you're feeling fancy add a wedge of orange. On special occasions swap the shitty wine out for prosecco.

Water

Despite the obvious fact that it isn't an alcoholic drink (if it burns like alcohol it's either vodka or poison, respond accordingly), it sits here as a reminder that water can provide a simple and refreshing option to help out the thirsty. After all, everyone needs water to hydrate after a long day and, y'know, to fucking survive. Note that, if you received this cookbook because of your poor kitchen performance, water is not likely to be adequate to appease your DGF and should never be used as an offering.

Water is best accompanied by frozen water (ice) and citrus fruit slices.

HOT DRINKS

It may come as a surprise but alcoholic drinks aren't for everyone or for every occasion. Your DFG may be unwell and in need of an alternative source of comfort and hydration. Hot drinks provide a very simple yet welcome solution.

Tea

Tea is probably the easiest hot drink to make. If you're failing in this endeavour then maybe you shouldn't be trusted near hot water. Put a tea bag in hot water until you think it tastes good. If unsure just leave the tea bag in and let the adults decide.

Coffee

If you have a coffee machine in your house, you should fucking know how to use it by now. No need for instructions here. If you don't know how to use the machine, walk the fuck away from it and use instant coffee and the kettle like a pleb.

Hot Chocolate

Hot chocolate always comes with instructions. Make sure you've got some milk and enough powder and then do what the instructions say. Include marshmallows on special occasions, when you're in the doghouse, or when marshmallows are on special.

*All we have is ingredients,
where's the food?*

BASIC COOKING STUFF

Congratulations, you've graduated from kitchen-illiterate to kitchen-initiate, or at least you're trusted enough to be allowed in the kitchen. The next steps in the *It's Your Fucking Turn To Cook* cookbook is to learn all the basics, and I mean basics. If you have trouble in this section you should seriously question your ability to survive without the assistance of a significant other.

Defrosting Meat

Meat does not last long before spoiling, but because meat is cheaper bought in bulk your DFG has probably created a stockpile that is kept in the freezer. Remove the meat from its package ensuring all the plastic is removed and put the meat on a plate. Check the net weight of the meat on the packaging, as this will be important.

All kitchen appliances (you know, the oven, dishwasher, blender, all of them) come with instructions. Follow the instructions on the microwave until the meat is defrosted. The advanced kitchen-initiate will plan the meal in advance and will shove the meat in the fridge well in advance to let it defrost over a day or so.

Boiling Things

Boiling water is a quick and easy way to cook some foods. Put water in a pot and heat on the stove. You will know that the water is hot enough when big bubbles start to form. Don't be a bellend and test the temperature of the water with your hand as it will hurt and you may require medical attention.

Toast

Oh, Honey!? You seriously don't know how to make toast? If that's the case you need to step out of the kitchen and never complain again about any food that is given to you. Remember to put the toaster away.

Peas and Corn

Peas and corn are an easy option for vegetables that can be found neatly packed in a plastic bag in the freezer. Sometimes with carrots. Take the packet from the freezer, and pour a reasonable amount into water to boil. Refer to the section *Boiling Things* if you need further instruction. Immediately return the bag to the freezer, as your DFG will not be happy to find it missing or defrosted into a ball of mush.

Advanced kitchen-initiates may attempt other green vegetables like broccoli or Brussels sprouts, or experiment with other utensils, such as a steamer.

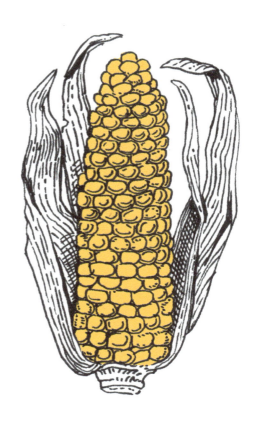

Premade Store-Bought Goodies

Even the most resourceful DFG will not be able to prepare every meal from scratch, and will make use of other options where necessary. The supermarket stocks a range of partially or fully prepared meals that any mug should be able to make use of. These meals conveniently come with preparation instructions on the packet, often in many languages including fourth grade English, so you have no excuse to go asking questions. If you do risk a question, you'd better have a *Double Offering* ready.

General Soup

Gather together a selection of hearty veggies. If you're not sure what counts as hearty veg, consult the pictures on any tin of soup you have handy. Then resist the urge to just use the tinned soup, you lazy bastard. Peel the vegetables, cut them into chunks and throw them in a pot. Pour in water up to the level of the veggies then cook on medium heat with a lid. That means not cold enough that nothing ever seems to happen and not hot enough that everything is boiling over and the smoke alarm is screaming at you.

Once everything is mushy, blitz the absolute bollocks out of it with a stick blender and serve with toast. For instructions see the *Toast* recipe.

Unspecified Meat and Noodle Soup

This is a good soup to have when you're crook. Dice all the veggies, which means cutting them into the rough size and shape of small dice. Boil until the water looks dirty. Throw in any precooked chunks of meat you like. Search up any noodles you have lying around, then chuck them in at the end and leave until noodles are cooked.

You then have a meat, noodle and veg soup. You can then name the soup based on whatever meat you've chucked in.

Pesto

One of the responsible adults in the house may have some herbs growing. If so, one of them is probably basil. Grab heaps of leaves off the basil plant if it's still alive. If it's dead we all know why, don't we. Blitz them using a stick blender along with garlic, olive oil, parmesan cheese and anything else you like until it looks like paste. Serve on cooked pasta or as a dip. If it will be sitting out for a bit make sure to add lemon juice so it doesn't darken to the colour of a dirty sponge.

Noodles

How the fuck did you manage to survive your early twenties without being able to prepare noodles? If you can't work out what to do, the instructions on the noodle packet are probably a good place to start. Fuck it, here's a recipe anyway. Boil the noodles until they seem cooked (Hint: once they're soft). If you're craving something more flavourful and substantial than the little sachet of MSG it comes with, fry up stuff like egg, onion or anything else you like in a pan while you're waiting. Mix it all together and eat it in quiet shame.

The slightly more adventurous amongst you can try to do the same with rice instead of noodles.

Stir Fry Veg

Tip the contents of your veggie crisper onto the bench and cut up any veg that takes your fancy. Then heat a pan on the stove to a high temperature. You're going to cook all of it in the one pan, but don't just throw it all in willy-nilly. There's a proper order to it, so pay attention.

First cook the onion, garlic and chilly-like things until it smells like spicy toffee.

Next throw in the harder veg that need to cook longer to soften up, like carrots and broccoli. Cook for a bit until it's all hot.

Then add the softer veg that will turn to mush if cooked too long, like zucchini, and cook until hot.

Finally add the leafy greens, like bok choy and spinach, and cook until they look sad and limp. If you've been clever enough to be boiling some noodles at the same time, whack them in now too.

Add whatever flavours you want (soy sauce, etc.) at the end.

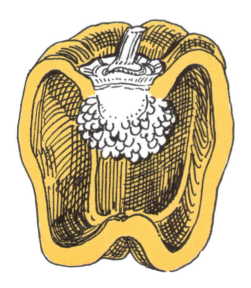
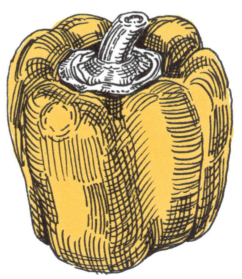

Freshly laid:

EGGS

Eggs. Sounds simple enough. We've all seen one, well I assume we all have. If not, eggs are the round objects that periodically pop out of chickens and other birds, which can then be cracked open and the insides used for food. They are incredibly pervasive so I would genuinely be surprised if you've never come across one and would wonder what sort of sheltered upbringing you've had. On the other hand, it may go some way to explain why you would require this sort of cookbook.

Boiled Egg

Boil water. Refer to the *Boiling Things* section if you need further instruction. Lower eggs in. Use the holey spoon from the drawer so you don't splash yourself with scalding water. Cook until hard enough for you, usually a few minutes. If the egg leaks, don't worry it will still cook fine, that's just the egg cracking up a bit.

Curried Egg

Take those *Boiled Eggs* once they're cooled enough for you to touch them all over. Peel off the shell and shove them in a bowl. You may need to rinse off any extra shell bits. Mash the fuckers up until it all blends into one colour. Whack in some curry powder and mayo until you're happy with the taste. Mix it all together. Serve in sandwiches with whatever.

Fried Egg

Make a fry pan hot. Once it's hot add some oil or spray depending on the pan. Time to crack new eggs from the fridge. If you're worried that you're going to fuck it up, crack them one at a time into a cup first and then pour onto the hot pan. Cook until it looks like a fried egg you've eaten before or seen on TV.

If you cock-up with the eggs, mix it all together, add whatever spices and pretend it was scrambled eggs all along. In that case serve with toast. If you've forgotten how to make toast, look back at the *Toast* recipe in this book.

Poached Egg

Put a heap of water in a pot and make it boil. Add some white vinegar (just a splash from the bottle). Crack an egg into a cup. Make sure the cup has a handle and isn't going to melt or crack in hot water. Lower the cup so a little bit of the boiling water can enter and cover the egg. Once that happens slowly tip the cup so that all the contents goes into the water. Leave for three minutes and then pull out with the holely spoon in the drawer. Drain the eggs on a crust of bread so they don't taste like vinegar.

Frittata/Omelette

Crack some number of eggs into a bowl and beat them until it's all the same colour. Four eggs is usually fine, but use as many as you need to fill a thick layer of whatever size pan you're going to use.

Add whatever veggies you like to the eggs, such as onion, zucchini, or anything that would cook easily and you think would taste good with eggs. Remember to cut them up and not just put a whole zucchini in the pan like a dimwit.

Spray or oil a pan so that things don't stick and heat it till it spits. Pour in all of the egg goop and cook until it looks like it will hold together. Flip it if you can to cook the other side.

If it all falls apart, that's fine. Mix the bugger up even more and pretend that you intended to make scrambled eggs. All good DFGs know that good home cooking is mostly about deception.

How long has that been there?

TINNED AND DRY FOOD

There are many things that can sit in the cupboard for ages and then still be cooked to make food. Unless of course there is something crawling in it, in that case you should consider those ingredients food for whatever is already eating it and don't even think about reclaiming it as human food, that's gross. You should know what to do with it. Toss it out. For the rest of the food that has managed to sit in the cupboard for a long time and still be good here are a couple of recipes to get you started.

Pasta Sauce

If you want to make a red pasta sauce from scratch chop some onions and garlic, and heat the fuckers in a pot until they look brown. Add tinned tomatoes and whatever dry flavours (chilli powder, dried herbs, and the like) you feel like to the pot. Boil it all until it's thick and looks like a sauce. If it's too thick and smells like burning you've used too much heat.

Once cooked, mix into cooked pasta (see the *Pasta* recipe) and add as much cheese as needed for flavour.

Pasta

Grab whatever bag of pasta from the cupboard and whatever sauce you can find in jars in the cupboard. These have all been premade or store bought. They're ready to go so you don't need to think about what's in there.

Heat the sauce in one pot with whatever meat you're using and perhaps some onions. Boil water in another pot. If you don't remember how to do that, look up **Boiling Things**. Add some salt to the water followed by the pasta. The instructions are on the label. Drain the pasta once it's soft and mix in with the sauce and whatever else you've decided to include.

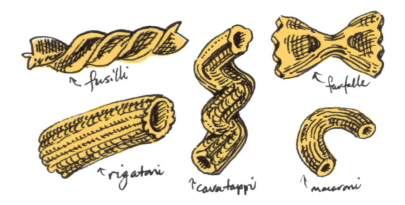

White Sauce

Melt a chunk of butter in a pot. Keep stirring the fucker.

Add plain flour to the butter until it is no longer a liquid. Keep stirring the fucker. You may at some point think that you can get away with not stirring. This is a mistake, as it will cause your sauce to stick and burn. It is not recommended to disturb your DFG with a smoke alarm. Add milk, a dash at a time. Keep stirring the fucker. Stop adding milk when it looks like thick cream.

Throw in as much cheese as you like. Keeps stirring the fucker.

The advance kitchen-initiate may attempt to add extras such as onion (at the start along with the butter) or chilli powder (at the end).

Tuna Pasta Salad

Cook pasta following the *Pasta* recipe. Let the bugger drain and cool, you don't want the pasta hot for this one. Open a tin of tuna. It's probably a good idea for you to search through the utensil drawer to find a can opener rather than try to bust that fucker open with just a knife. Use a colander, which looks like a bowl with holes in it, to drain the liquid out of the tuna. Mix the pasta and tuna together in a bowl along with a bit of salt and olive oil. Add any number of extras to fill out the salad (think chickpeas, red onion, baby spinach, capsicum).

Pastry

Are you sure you actually want to try this one? It's not really hard, but no one is going to mind if you just buy it from the shop. You won't get brownie points for making it from scratch. Fine. Here we go then.

Put flour in the blender so it's about half full. Add chunks of butter and keep blending, one chunk at a time until it looks and feels like coarse sand.

Add water to the mixture a bit at a time and rub it about until it feels like playdough. Make it into a ball, wrap in plastic and shove it in the fridge for a short while. Once it feels like a soft chilled brick, roll it out into the shape you want. Sprinkle flour on the bench to stop it from sticking. Fit your pastry into whatever tins you're using then bake at 180 degrees Celsius until golden and crispy. Go by feel. It should then be ready to add any filling you like.

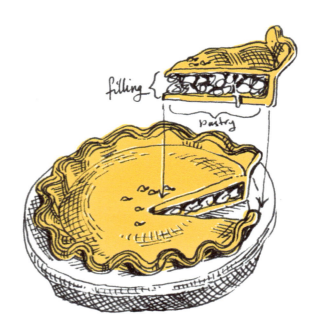

Hollandaise Sauce

Hollandaise sauce is a relatively easy way to look like you're fancy and know your way around a kitchen by making something that you can get in a jar from the supermarket. It will however give your wrist quite a workout, so don't masturbate beforehand.

Get 250g of butter (read the packaging to work out how to do this) and cut into chunks (small ones). Have these ready to go.

Put three egg yolks (that's the yellow part) into a glass bowl that says it's microwave safe. Fill a pot with water and have it steaming on the stove like a nice hot tea. Pop the bowl on top, but don't let it touch the water or you will fry your eggs.

Add one chunk of butter to the bowl and stir the fucker with a whisk until that chunk of butter completely melts. Then add the next chunk and repeat. Keep going until all the butter is melted.

Add however much lemon juice you like and let it cool. Now that you know how it's made you might feel weird about putting it on your eggs, but don't worry about it too much. This is why it's not called egg sauce to put on eggs.

Does this smell right?

USING FRESHISH STUFF

Bowls of fruits and vegetables are beautiful to look at and gives a room a homely and fresh feeling. What you might not realise is that this fresh produce can also be used to make food. If the idea of eating such fresh ingredients is a new and unfamiliar concept for you then I imagine you may have some questions, though I think you'd be better off asking a doctor. In the meantime you need to get some honest fresh food into your system. Let's get that started.

47]

Does it smell?

Your first task in the kitchen will often be to separate food from what is no longer food. Does it smell rank? Does it look like a mound of slush? Then don't fucking use it. If it's vegetables feed it to the worms. If it's not toss in the correct bin.

Roast

Shove the defrosted meat on a tray and into the oven at 180 degrees Celsius. See the *Defrosting Meat* recipe to help get you going.

Throw whatever veggies are in the fridge and/or cupboards (mostly potatoes, carrots and the like) onto a tray with oil and shove it in the oven. Check in on them about every twenty minutes and toss them with a wooden spoon. Make sure nothing is burning while you're there. If something is burning remove it from the oven and leave the rest to keep cooking.

You can stab the meat to see how cooked it is. If you are unsure think about all the other fucking roasts you've eaten and what they looked like and try to cook it until it looks the same.

Salad

A good rule of thumb for salad is to use whatever's available. Most of that should be green shit like lettuce, or maybe baby spinach if you want to be fancy, but some other colours are nice in the mix too. Wash all of it, drain it, make them into bite size pieces, and put it in something to serve. Sprinkle with salt, then red vinegar of some sort and then olive oil. If it's all sitting in a pool of liquid, you've used too much.

Steamed Veg

Put a steamer into a pot with some water. For the kitchen-illiterate, a steamer is a vessel or utensil with holes in the bottom to allow steam in. Not to be confused with a strainer, which has holes in the bottom to let water out. Add whatever veg needs using up. Cook until it's ready. Carrot usually needs a wee bit longer than the other veggies.

Mashed Potato

Peel potatoes. Cut into chunks. Make it small chunks if you want your mashed potato quicker. Boil the fuck out of it until the pieces start to fall apart. Use the *Boiling Things* recipe to get you going. Drain the potatoes. Put the potato back into the pot. Mash the fucker and add the whatever butter, milk and salt you feel like. If your hipster friends think it's too pedestrian tell them it's smashed potato instead.

Barbecue

Grab whatever meat is available, defrost if needed following the *Defrosting Meat* recipe. You know how the barbeque process goes, you've done it many times before at social events. Pick up some utensils and go to town. Don't worry about the salads, because somehow working the barbeque exempts you from doing everything else. Grab yourself a beer while you're at it too, because apparently never setting foot in a kitchen and then occasionally manning the barbeque means you deserve an *Offering*. Beware asking anything of your DFG who's spent days organising the whole event, especially if you're holding a beer. Any questions will require a *Double Offering*.

Stew

This is a useful recipe for getting rid of anything from the fridge that needs using up. Grab out all the aging root veggies and almost empty sauce bottles. Rinse the bottles out and use that water for the stew. Use the big fuck-off pot probably found at the back of the cupboard. Put in all the chopped meat and veg you want. Add a tin of diced tomatoes and then enough water so you can just see it rise through everything else. Put it on the stove at a very low temperature. I mean very low. Now fuck off for four to five hours and let it all cook. Test it every now and then if you feel like it, to see if it's cooked and to make sure that it hasn't burnt to the bottom and destroyed another pot.

Bread

Put two cups of normal flour in a bowl. Put some dry yeast (you'll find it in the freezer or in packets with instructions on it. I'll pretend you know what to do with instructions) and sugar in along with it. The amount of yeast should be matched by the amount of sugar. For a more fluffy, yeast flavoured loaf use more yeast and sugar. Add some salt and pepper if you feel like it.

Stir all the dry stuff together. Add warm water and mix it all together until it feels like a lump of glue. Throw it onto a floured bench then punch and fold the fucker while adding more flour so that it doesn't stick to you so much. Keep going until it feels like a neat, firm ball of dough. Put that into a bowl and cover with glad wrap (the entire bowl, not just the dough). Leave it for a while to rise.

Once your dough looks twice the size, throw it back on the bench and manhandle it into shape to fit your bread tin. Bake it in the oven at 180 degrees Celsius until it looks a wee bit darker than bread bought from the store.

Pizza

This feels like we're going out on a limb here but let's see how this fucking thing goes.

Do the *Bread* recipe but rather than shape it to the bread tin, roll it out flat to make pizza bases. Don't fret if it isn't perfectly round, pizza shops these days use a machine to get that consistent shape. I take no responsibility for any mess you make in attempting the toss and spin method.

Put that flat bread into the oven for about ten minutes until it kind of feels like it's crusty, but only a bit not proper crusty. Pull it out of the oven and then add whatever toppings you like. The sauce is always on the bottom and the cheese is always on the top and the rest is literally anything else you like and/or needs eating up.

Shove it back in a hot over (180-200 degrees Celsius depending on how you feel) until the cheese is bubbling and a wee bit brown at the edges.

Cut it up and you're done.

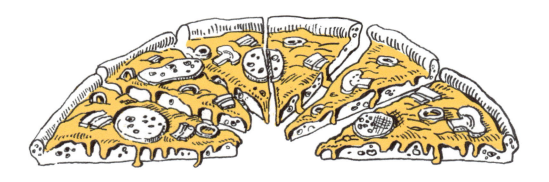

Gnocchi

Use the *Mashed Potato* recipe, except this time don't add any of the whatevers and instead just let the potatoes cool. Mash the fuckers up, adding a couple of eggs, salt and pepper. Then stir in enough flour so that it looks like playdough. Roll chunks of that fucker into bite-size pieces.

Bring a pot of water to boil, and I mean boil, and then pop a couple of chunks in at a time. You'll know they're cooked when they float. Pull them out to drain using that holey spoon in the drawer and add more potato chunks to the boiling water.

Once you've done the lot mix all those chunks into a pasta sauce.

Burnt Spice Nachos

Seriously? If someone thinks you need this book, there's no way you're ready to attempt this dish. If you are feeling game, you should phone a friend.

Crumbed Meat

Get meat, defrost it if you have to following the *Defrosting Meat* recipe. Lay it out on a plate and sprinkle plain flour over top. It should cover most of the meat.

In a bowl beat the crap out of an egg until it looks all the same colour.

In a separate bowl pour some bread crumbs. It might also be handy to have a spare plate at the end of the line to put the crumbed meat on.

One at a time, dip the floured meat in the egg so that it is wet all over. Then smack it around in the crumbs until it is covered.

Once all done with all the meat, fry the fuckers in some hot oil until they are cooked through like meat normally should be. If the crumbs are black there's too much heat happening. Turn it down, you twit.

If you bang the meat a few times with a mallet before you crumb it, then you've got schnitzel.

Salmon

Fishing as a pastime is more of a convenient means of getting the kitchen-illiterate out from under a DFG's feet than a source of food. But if you insist that fish is something you actually want to eat, I recommend sourcing it from the market. Salmon is a good option as they come in steak-like fillets, even though they'd be pretty fucking weird looking steaks.

The convenience of fish, rather than in catching it, is in the cooking, as it's pretty fucking quick and easy to do. Make some cooking device or other hot, then whack those puppies in/on there. On the stove, turn after about 6 minutes and cook for a similar length of time. In the oven, 10 minutes at a decent temperature is usually plenty.

Once cooked, pop those suckers on plates and sprinkle with whatever's handy (salt, pepper, lemon juice, shit like that).

Bubble 'n' Squeak

This is a time-honoured recipe that will bring back childhood memories and hopefully not even shatter them. Bubble 'n' Squeak is just chopping up leftovers and heating them in a pan.

Hurry the fuck up, then. That might have sounded like a description but it was an instruction. Add some oil while you're at it or the fucker will stick to the pan and you'll be stuck cleaning the bastard afterwards and you'll have wasted all the time you saved by frying up leftovers in the first place. Heat until hot. If there's veggies in there a nice crispy edge is good. Serve on clean plates and pretend that it's a brand new meal. If you're feeling fancy add any whatevers to mix up the flavours a bit.

Ifits

For those times when you can't be arsed cooking and every other person in the household is capable of putting food in their mouth hole but are using it to whinge about what to eat, you may want to invoke an Ifit protocol. If you're game and have the forethought to hide all the treats you want to keep for yourself, then the process is quite simple: if it's there, they can eat it. Make sure you don't fuck it up and forget to also hide your DFG's favourite treats, especially the kind of thing you might otherwise use as an offering. In fact, you should probably go and serve Ifits up to your DFG yourself, just to be on the safe side.

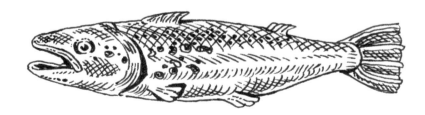

Where to finish:

SWEET THINGS

The majority of foods so far in this cookbook have been mains. You know, the big part of the meal that is supposed to be filling and provide enough sustenance to last until the next main meal. Sometimes this isn't enough and a little sweet is warranted. Or other times you may want to show off with a surprise dessert. Don't go straight to the tub of ice cream hidden in the freezer. This next section has some foods that you can try instead, and potentially serve with the ice cream.

Stewed Fruit

Cut the blasted fruit up and put it in a pot. Add a wee bit of water and then a fuckton of sugar. Heat and stir until it's all sloppy and would look good with ice cream. If you leave it on for too long let it continue for a little longer and pretend it's jam.

Whipped Cream

Grab some cream from the fridge. You know, the thickish white goop that has been mentioned in half the dessert recipes. Put however much you want into a bowl. Make sure the bowl is big enough or you'll make a huge mess that you'll have to clean up. Use something that beats things. I'd recommend something electronic to save a heap of time. Whip the cream until it's thicker and looks like whipped cream. For flair add vanilla or icing sugar.

Stewed Fruit Crumble

Use the *Stewed Fruit* recipe to make the base. Add cornflakes. You now have stewed fruit crumble. Add cream or ice cream. If you're feeling saucy, add both.

Banana Bread

The wet things can go straight into the blender: two old peeled bananas as brown as you like, some melted butter, a cup of milk and two eggs. Blend those fuckers until they're sauce.

The dry things should be stirred together in a bowl: two-and-a-half cups of self-raising flour, one cup of normal flour and a cup of brown sugar. Mix them together and then mix the wet stuff in too. It should look like a thick batter once you're done.

Shove it all into a bread tray that you've sprayed the fuck out of so it doesn't stick. Put it into the oven that is preheated to 180 degrees Celsius. Leave it in there for 40 minutes or so. Stab the fucker with a knife, if it comes out clean you're done. If not leave it in there until the knife comes out clean.

Pancakes

Start with two eggs and crack them into a bowl. Add equal parts of self-raising and plain flour until you're happy and mix the eggs through. It will all just form a thick mess, this is fine. Add milk in small amounts and mix until it looks and feels like a batter.

Make a non-stick pan hot and cook the batter in flat pieces. As the pancake cooks the batter will form bubbles, and these will eventually burst and become holes. Only then should you attempt to flip it. If the temperature is too hot you should smell and see the burning. If the first pancake comes out pretty crap, don't worry about it, this always happens.

Self-Saucing Pudding

This should be fun. If you screw it up just make sure the pudding bit is cooked and then drown it in golden syrup or cream and pretend it wasn't meant to be a self-saucing pudding in the first place.

Mix the dry and wet stuff separately and then stir them in together. The dry stuff is one and a bit cups of self-raising flour, half a cup of brown sugar, and half a cup of cocoa powder. The wet stuff is one egg, one cup of milk, and a thin chunk of melted butter.

Mix all the ingredients together until it looks like a dark batter. Spray the fuck out of an oven pan and put the batter in it.

Sprinkle a cup of brown sugar over top. Very, oh god, very gently pour a cup of boiling water on top. It will make it look like a swamp but that's fine. If you pour too fast you'll blast a hole in the batter like an amateur and this is not what you want.

Shove it in the oven, which should already be at 180 degrees Celsius. Cook for however long it needs, say 20 minutes. Poke its guts with a stick. If batter sticks to it, put it back in for a bit. If it doesn't it's ready to go.

Serve with cold creamy stuff.

Fuck! They're here. Now what?

DEALING WITH GUESTS

We all have friends, or at least people who feel comfortable enough around us to occasionally visit. They could arrive without warning, or more likely, they arrive as you had planned but completely forgotten about. Your DFG should no longer have to whip up a delicious last-minute meal so that you don't look like an idiot who completely forgot your friends and family. Now you can do that all by yourself with this handy guide on dealing with guests.

Drinks

Ask what they want and put plenty out. Take wine from the bottles you're allowed to touch or whatever is already open and still tastes like wine.

Potato Chips

Head off to the servo and buy a few packets or use what's in the cupboard. Put them into a bowl. Make sure the big open part of the bowl faces upwards. Share with the crowd.

Cheeses

As long as it smell like cheese, put it on a plate and share with crackers.

'Tasty' is not a legitimate type of cheese. But if that's all you've got in the fridge, chop it into cubes and serve with pickles or something so people think it looks fancier.

Popcorn

This is a fun snack to have when watching TV and is easily whipped up for guests. You can add whatever flavour you like to these little suckers.

Use any oil but olive oil. Put it in a pot that has a lid, enough to cover the bottom of the pot. Make that oil fucking hot. Add the popcorn kernels and shake it over the heat until those fuckers start popping and keep going until they're not popping anymore.

Put it in a bowl and add whatever flavour you think would work.

Hummus

Shove a drained tin of chickpeas into the blender, along with a bit of garlic and sesame seeds. Go by taste for the extra whatevers you feel like. Blend the fuck out of it. Mix in some olive oil and lemon juice until it's shiny. Serve with something so people don't have to use their fingers to get it in them.

Tomato Dip

Throw a tin of diced tomatoes (kind of drained) into a blender with a peeled onion and some garlic. Blend the fuck out of it. Add whatever (chilly, basil, oregano, whatever the fuck you feel like or just happens to be growing in your garden, just to add taste). Serve with bread or crackers.

For the Rest

Use an app. Order the sucker in.

If you need to show off, book a table elsewhere and take everyone to that place for dinner.

If you can't afford to eat out, barbecue whatever meat you have in the fridge/freezer and tell someone to bring salad. See the Barbecue recipe to get you started.

Where was that fucking recipe again?

Index/List of Recipes

An index section seems straightforward but one can never tell. You've done well to get this far in the book. It shows that you are at least panic-flicking through these pages to try and find something to cook that won't get you in trouble. With a handy index section you don't have to flick very far. All the recipes are listed alphabetically, that's A to Z, next to the page number

INDEX

Banana Bread, 61
Barbecue, 50
Boiled Egg, 34
Boiling Things, 24
Bread, 51
Bubble 'n' Squeak, 55
Burnt Spice Nachos, 53
Cheeses, 68
Coffee, 19
Crumbed Meat, 54
Curried Egg, 34
Drinks, 13
Defrosting Meat, 24
Fried Egg, 34
Frittata, 35
Gnocchi, 53
Hollandaise Sauce, 43
Hummus, 69
Ifits, 55
Mashed Potato, 49
Noodles, 27
Omelette, 35
Pancakes, 62
Pasta, 40
Pasta Sauce, 40
Pastry, 42
Peas and Corn, 25
Pesto, 27
Pizza, 52
Poached Egg, 35

Popcorn, 68
Potato Chips, 68
Premade Store-Bought Goodies, 25
Roast, 48
Salad, 48
Salmon, 54
Self-Saucing Pudding, 63
Soup, 26
Steamed Veg, 49
Stew, 50
Stewed Fruit, 60
Stewed Fruit Crumble, 60
Stir Fry Veg, 29
Tea, 18
Toast, 24
Tomato Dip, 69
Tuna Pasta Salad, 41
Whipped Cream, 60
White Sauce, 41
Wines, 16

Lightning Source UK Ltd.
Milton Keynes UK
UKHW020810131021
392025UK00003B/192